I Thank God for You, Mom
Copyright 2002 by Zondervan
ISBN 0-310-80314-4

Requests for information should be addressed to:
Inspirio, The gift group of Zondervan
Grand Rapids, Michigan 49530
http://www.inspiriogifts.com

Compiler and Project Manager: Molly C. Detweiler
Design: Kris Nelson
Cover Photo: Comstock Images

Printed in China
02 03 04/HK/ 4 3 2 1

I Thank God for You, Mom

inspirio™

The gift group of Zondervan

Mother

You filled my days with rainbow lights,
Fairy tales and sweet dream nights,
A kiss to wipe away my tears,
Gingerbread to ease my fears.

You gave the gift of life to me
And then in love, you set me free.
I thank you for your tender care,
For deep warm hugs and being there.

I hope that when you think of me
A part of you
You'll always see.

AUTHOR UNKNOWN

Many women do noble things,

but you surpass them all.

Mothers hold their children's hands for a few years, but their hearts forever.

ANCIENT SAYING

*W*hat a blessing you've been to me, Mom. You blessed me with your time, your knowledge, your prayers, but most of all, with your unconditional love!

B

*T*he Lord bless you and keep you;
the Lord make his face shine upon you
and be gracious to you;
the Lord turn his face toward you
and give you peace.

NUMBERS 6:24–26

Maternal love: a miraculous substance which God multiplies as He divides it.

VICTOR HUGO

*G*od gives us friends—and that means much; but far above all others, the greatest of his gifts to earth was when he thought of mothers.

ANONYMOUS

*M*om, I pray that my heart will be filled with love for others, just as yours was for me. You never stopped loving me, no matter what. I want to be like that, too.

A Mother's Love

There are times when only a Mother's love
Can understand our tears,
Can soothe our disappointments
And calm all of our fears.

There are times when only a Mother's love
Can share the joy we feel
When something we've dreamed about
Quite suddenly is real.

There are times when only a Mother's faith
Can help us on life's way
And inspire in us the confidence
We need from day to day.

For a Mother's heart and a Mother's faith
And a Mother's steadfast love
Were fashioned as the angels'
And sent from God above.

AUTHOR UNKNOWN

You Were There

You were there when we took our first steps,
And went unsteadily across the floor.
You pushed and prodded: encouraged and guided,
Until our steps took us out the door.

You worry now "Are they okay?"
Is there more you could have done?
As we walk the paths of our unknown
You wonder "Where have my children gone?"

Where we are is where you have led us,
With your special love you showed us a way,
To believe in ourselves and the decisions we make.
Taking on the challenge of life day-to-day.

And where we go you can be sure,
In spirit you shall never be alone.
For where you are is what matters most to us,
Because to us that will always be home.

AUTHOR UNKNOWN

The mother's heart
is the child's schoolroom.

HENRY WARD BEECHER

Teach children how they should live,
and they will remember it all their life.

PROVERBS 22:6 GNT

The great academy, a mother's knee.

THOMAS CARLYLE

I thank God
for your teaching, Mom,
that showed me the way to go.

*P*ride is one of the seven deadly sins;
but it cannot be the pride of a mother in
her children, for that is a compound of
two cardinal virtues—faith and hope.

CHARLES DICKENS

*L*et your father and mother be proud
of you; give your mother that happiness.

PROVERBS 23:25 GNT

*M*ay my words and
actions always make you
proud to be my mother!

Mom, it was you who made our house a home... a place I always wanted to come back to. It wasn't just that you made sure it was clean and comfortable, or that you scented the air with cinnamon and the smells of good food, or even that you decorated with our photos and various macaroni and finger paint masterpieces. It was that you were there, always, with open arms and love that never failed. That is what made our house a home for me.

With all my heart, I thank you, Mom.

I Love You, Mom!

Mom's smiles can brighten any moment,
Mom's hugs put joy in all our days,
Mom's love will stay with us forever
and touch our lives in precious ways.

The values you've taught,
the care you've given,
and the wonderful love you've shown,
have enriched my life,
and blessed my days
in more ways than can be known.
I love you, Mom!

AUTHOR UNKNOWN

$\mathcal{A}$ mother's arms are made of tenderness and children sleep soundly in them.

VICTOR HUGO

$\mathcal{A}$ rich child often sits in a poor mother's lap.

SPANISH PROVERB

Mother

if it wasn't for your prayers

and your guidance,

I don't know

where I'd be!

I was young
and now I am old,
yet I have never seen
the righteous forsaken
or their children begging bread.
They are always generous and
lend freely; their children will be blessed.

PSALM 37:25–26

*I*n many ways, mothers are like sculptors. Through their
love and gentle guidance, they mold "little characters"
into adults *with* character!

*L*isten ... to your father's instruction and do not forsake
your mother's teaching. They will be a garland to grace your
head and a chain to adorn your neck.

PROVERBS 1:8–9

My Mother

When sleep forsook my open eye,
Who was it sung sweet lullaby
And rocked me that I should not cry?
My mother.

Who ran to help me when I fell
And would some pretty story tell,
Or kiss the part to make it well?
My mother.

Who taught my infant lips to pray,
To love God's holy word and day,
And walk in wisdom's pleasant ways?
My mother.

And I can never cease to be
Affectionate and kind to thee
Who was so very kind to me—
my Mother.

JANE TAYLOR

The LORD blesses the home of the righteous.

PROVERBS 3:33

*M*ost Wonderful

*O*verwhelmingly Sweet

*T*errifically Gifted

*H*eart Pure as Gold

*E*ver Patient and Caring

*R*esponsible for So Much Joy

MOLLY C. DETWEILER

17

One day, while home visiting my parents, I happened to pass by my mother's open jewelry box. There were no large sparkling diamonds or creamy strings of pearls. There were however, handmade cards with childish scribbles on them, yellowed with time. Beside them were a couple macaroni necklaces, their gold spray painted veneer chipping with age. And, placed carefully in a spot all its own, was a cheap heart shaped locket opened to display the dimpled faces of two babies, who were now adults.

Thank you, Mom, for seeing me as a treasure, just as you are an incredible treasure to me.

Those who plan what is good find love and faithfulness.

Mom, thank you, for never doubting that I could be a success at whatever I tried. Because of your confidence in me, I was able to try lots of new things and learn about my gifts and talents. I owe much of what I am today to you and your steadfast belief in me.

Mother means selfless devotion, limitless sacrifice, and love that passes understanding.

AUTHOR UNKNOWN

Mom, thank you for loving me, just because I'm yours and not because of anything I do. You help me better understand the unconditional love of God.

Mother love is like God's love;
He loves us not because we are lovable,
but because it is His nature to love, and
because we are His children.

EARL RINEY

You are one of the ways God gave his grace to me. Thank you for allowing God to use you to make my life so rich.

How great is the love the Father has lavished on us, that we should be called children of God! And that is what we are!

1 JOHN 3:1

From the fullness of God's grace we have all received one blessing after another.

JOHN 1:16

I Thank God for You, Mom,
Because...

You walked around the house all night

with me when I wouldn't stop crying.

You showed up at work with spit-up in your hair,

milk stains on your blouse and diapers in your purse.

You had the amazing ability to nurse me, cook dinner,

and sew a button on a shirt, all at the same time.

You read "Goodnight, Moon" twice a night for a year.

And then read it again because I begged:

"Just one more time?"

You ran carpools and made cookies

and sewed school play costumes.

Your heart ached a little when you

watched me disappear down the street,

walking to school alone for the very first time.

Because...

You froze your buns off sitting on metal bleachers at football or soccer games on Friday nights instead of watching from your car, so that when I asked, "Did you see me?" you could say, "Of course, I wouldn't have missed it for the world." And you meant it.

You bit your lip instead of saying what you wanted to when I was 14 and dyed my hair green.

You had patience and compassion without limit.

When it was time, you let me go, even though that ached a lot more.

Mostly, though, I thank God for you because you're mine, and because I know you'll always, always love me.

AUTHOR UNKNOWN

Thank you, Mom, for helping me to face my fears through your love and care. You were there to reassure me that I was safe when the storm was raging outside my window. Whenever you were near, I knew that I didn't have to be afraid. Now, even though you can't always be by my side when the storms of life are raging, the memory of your love helps me have confidence that I will be safe.

There is no fear in love. Perfect love drives out fear.

1 JOHN 4:18

A godly mother mirrors God's love.
Thank you for reflecting God's love
into my life!

DORIS RIKKERS

May you be blessed by the LORD,
the Maker of heaven and earth.

PSALM 115:15

A mother's love

is a glimpse of heaven.

ELIZABETH BECK

Little Things

Little drops of water
    Little grains of sand,
Make the mighty ocean
    And the pleasant land.

Thus the little moments,
    Humble though they be
Make the mighty ages
    Of eternity.

Little deeds of kindness,
    Little words of love,
Make our earth an Eden,
    Like the heaven above.

JULIA A. F. CARNEY

Mom,

It was the little things you did for me, and continue to do, that make me smile when I think of you. Little things like…

Throwing snowballs with me after the first big snow, even when you had "more important" things to do.

Letting me help you plant flowers with my little hands, even when it would have been easier and faster to do it alone.

Getting me that puppy that became my best friend and feeding it every day because I always forgot.

Making me a birthday cake with whatever I wanted on it every year, no matter how bizarre the request ("This year I want an apple tree on my cake. An apple tree that grows pickles!")

Scraping together the money to buy me the prom dress I so desperately wanted, along with the pretty shoes and jewelry.

Sending me care packages when I was in college full of microwave popcorn, those chewy fruit snacks I love, and warm socks … just to say "I love you."

The list of the little things could stretch for miles. Thanks for all of them. You've always made me feel so loved!

MOLLY C. DETWEILER

$\mathcal{M}$ost beautiful things in life come by twos and threes, by dozens and hundreds. Plenty of roses, stars, sunsets, rainbows, brothers and sisters, aunts and cousins, but only one mother in the whole world.

KATE DOUGLAS WIGGIN

I'm so thankful that you are my one and only mother!

*M*ay every child in need
find as dear a mother as mine.
May they hear a voice
as kind as yours—
a voice that I still love to hear!

ADAPTED FROM ROBERT LOUIS STEVENSON

A Blessing

*M*ay God bless you always ...
For the long nights you lay awake,
watching over me in sickness,
or praying for me through troubles.
For your comforting hand that held mine tight
and led me through an uncertain world.
For all the storybooks you read.
For all the pains you comforted.

Thank you, Mother, for showing me what God is like in your loving words and actions. You came to me with a healing touch when I was sick, and no one else wanted to be with me. You cheered me on and gave me confidence through your encouragement, even when everyone else said I couldn't do it.
You listened to my hurts and confusion and offered wise counsel, when all others would have led me astray.
You never turned me away when I came asking forgiveness, even when I had hurt you to the depths of your heart.
You have always loved me unconditionally, even though I'm not always very lovable.

For all the many ways you have shown me heavenly love, I can't thank you enough!

The righteous will flourish like a palm tree, they will
grow like a cedar of Lebanon; planted in the house of
the Lord, they will flourish in the courts of our God.

PSALM 92:12–13

Thank you, Mom,

For all your love

For teaching me

About God above

For helping me to

Learn and grow

For all these things

I love you so!

Mother Knows Best

A mother understands that her little child would like to have only candy for supper or stay out all night as a teenager. She is careful to prevent that from happening even though she knows it would make her child happy for a time. And every mother wants her children to be happy. Then why does the mother not want her child to have what he or she wants? Why does she work so hard to help her children make the right decisions? If she wants a happy child, then it makes little sense to deny it the very thing it wants.

She knows a moment's pleasure gorging on candy will end with a major stomachache. She knows that the fun of staying out all night could end in tragedy or at the very least, will be unhealthy. The child's unhappiness when they have to face the consequences will be equal to its delight now. She is guiding the child away from those pleasures that will only bring tears. Passing joys can leave us with bitterness. What a blessing and gift from God it is to have a wise mother who will guide us away from the instant gratifications that ultimately bring regret.

ADAPTED FROM GUIGO THE FIRST

A Mother's love

endures through all.

WASHINGTON IRVING

*L*ove is patient, love is kind.

It does not envy, it does not boast, it is not proud.

It is not rude, it is not self-seeking, it is not easily angered,

it keeps no record of wrongs. Love does not delight in evil

but rejoices with the truth. It always protects, always trusts,

always hopes, always perseveres. Love never fails.

1 CORINTHIANS 13:4–8

When a child was asked, "Where is your home?" she replied, "Wherever my mother is, is my home."

AUTHOR UNKNOWN

For all the times you stayed up
> When my tummy was upset

And all the nights you made up
> Stories, because I wasn't sleepy yet

For all the things you gave up
> To make sure my needs were met

Mom, this little girl you raised up ...

Will never, ever your love forget!

MOLLY C. DETWEILER

The prayer of a good person has a powerful effect.

JAMES 5:16 GNT

When the world makes you feel unworthy, Mom, remember: A hundred years from now it will not matter what was in your bank account, or the sort of house you lived in, or the kind of car you drove. But the world will be different because you were important in the life of a child—this child. Thank you, Mom!

Most of the stones for the buildings of the City of God, and all of the best of them, are made by mothers.

HENRY DRUMMOND

As I Look Back ...

As I look back on my life

I find myself wondering ...

Did I remember to thank you

for all that you have done for me?

For all of the times you were by my side

to help me celebrate my successes

and accept my defeats?

Or for teaching me the value of hard work

good judgment, courage, and honesty?

I wonder if I've ever thanked you

for the simple things ...

The laughter, smiles, and quiet times we've shared?

If I have forgotten to express my gratitude

For any of these things,

I am thanking you now ...

and I am hoping that you've known all along,

how very much you are loved and appreciated.

AUTHOR UNKNOWN

A Precious Mother

Mom, you've given me so much:

Love from your heart,

The warmth of your touch,

The gift of life

and you're a friend to me.

We have a very Special Bond

which only comes from God;

I'm sure you agree.

As a child I would say "Mommy, I love you,"

Now you're my Mother so dear

I love you even more

with each and every new year.

If I could have chosen,

I would have picked no other

Than for you to be my lifelong friend

and Precious Mother.

AUTHOR UNKNOWN

How hard it is to find
a capable wife!
She is worth far more than jewels!
Her husband puts his confidence in her,
and he will never be poor.
As long as she lives,
she does him good and never harm.
She keeps herself busy
making wool and linen cloth.
She brings home food from out-of-the-way places,
as merchant ships do.
She gets up before daylight to prepare food for her family
and to tell her servant women what to do.
She looks at land and buys it,
and with money she has earned she plants a vineyard.
She is a hard worker,
strong and industrious.
She knows the value of everything she makes,
and works late into the night.
She spins her own thread
and weaves her own cloth.
She is generous to the poor and needy.

She doesn't worry when it snows,

because her family has warm clothing.

She makes bedspreads

and wears clothes of fine purple linen.

Her husband is well known,

one of the leading citizens.

She makes clothes and belts,

and sells them to merchants.

She is strong and respected

and not afraid of the future.

She speaks with a gentle wisdom.

She is always busy

and looks after her family's needs.

Her children show their appreciation,

and her husband praises her.

He says, "Many women are good wives,

but you are the best of them all."

Charm is deceptive and beauty disappears,

but a woman who honors the Lord

should be praised.

Give her credit for all she does.

She deserves the respect of everyone.

PROVERBS 31:10–31 GNT

I saw you hang my first painting on the refrigerator,
and I wanted to paint another one.

When you thought I wasn't looking,
I saw you feed a stray cat,
and I thought it was good to be kind to animals.

When you thought I wasn't looking,
I saw you make my favorite cake for me,
and I knew that little things are special things.

When you thought I wasn't looking,
I heard you pray, and I believed there that
God was someone I could always talk to.

When you thought I wasn't looking,
I felt you kiss me good night, and I felt loved.

When you thought I wasn't looking,
I saw tears come from your eyes,
and I learned that sometimes things hurt,
and it's all right to cry.

When you thought I wasn't looking,
I saw you give to someone needy and
I learned the joy of giving.

When you thought I wasn't looking,
I saw you always did your best
and it made me want to be all that I could be.

When you thought I wasn't looking,
I heard you say "thank you" and
I wanted to say thanks to you for all the things
I saw when you thought I wasn't looking.

AUTHOR UNKNOWN

*B*eing a full time mother is one of the highest salaried jobs for the payment you receive is pure love.

MILDRED B. VERMONT

Life began with waking up and loving my mother's face.

GEORGE ELIOT

A Mother

is a person who seeing

there are only four pieces

of pie and five people promptly

announced she never did care for pie.

TENNEVA JORDAN

*O*ne thing God has spoken, two things have I heard:

that you, O God, are strong, and that you, O Lord,

are loving. Surely you will reward each person according to

what he has done.

PSALM 62:11–12

My Mother

My Mother, my friend so dear
throughout my life you're always near.
A tender smile to guide my way
You're the sunshine to light my day.

AUTHOR UNKNOWN

Thank you, Mom, for
"reading my mind" so many times;
you understood my sadness
when I couldn't speak through my tears,
and you understood my joy
when all I could do was laugh and sing.

The memory of the righteous will be a blessing.

PROVERBS 10:7

A mother understands what a child does not say.

AUTHOR UNKNOWN

I Said a Mother's Prayer for You

I said a Mother's prayer for you

to thank the Lord above

for blessing me with a lifetime

of your tenderhearted love.

I thanked God for the caring

you've shown me through the years,

for the closeness we've enjoyed

in time of laughter and of tears.

And so, I thank you from the heart

for all you've done for me

and I bless the Lord for giving me

the best mother there could be!

AUTHOR UNKNOWN

May the Lord repay you
for what you have done.
May you be richly rewarded
by the Lord.

RUTH 2:12